POEMS FOR HUNGRY *Souls*

101 SPIRITUAL POEMS

POEMS FOR HUNGRY Souls

101 SPIRITUAL POEMS

JEANNIE COLON

BMcTALKS Press
4980 South Alma School Road
Suite 2-493
Chandler, Arizona 85248

Copyright © 2020 by Jeannie Colon. All rights reserved.

No part of this publication may be reproduced, stored in a retrieval system, or transmitted in any form or by any means, electronic, mechanical, photocopying, recording, scanning, or otherwise without the prior written permission of the Publisher. Requests to the Publisher for permissions should be submitted to the Permissions Department, BMcTALKS Press, 4980 S. Alma School Road, Ste 2-493, Chandler, AZ 85248 or at www.bmctalkspress.com/permissions

The views expressed in this publication are those of the author; are the responsibility of the author; and do not necessarily reflect or represent the views of BMcTALKS Press, its owner, or its independent contractors.

Scripture quotations are taken from the New International Version (NIV). Holy Bible, New International Version®, NIV® Copyright © 1973, 1978, 1984, 2011 by Biblica, Inc.® Used by permission. All rights reserved worldwide.

Scripture quotations are taken from the New King James Version (NKJV) Copyright © 1982 by Thomas Nelson. Used by permission. All rights reserved.

Unless otherwise noted in the text, scripture quotations have been taken from NKJV.

Volume pricing is available to bulk orders placed by corporations, associations, and others. For details, please contact BMcTALKS Press at info@bmtpress.com

FIRST EDITION

Library of Congress Control Number: 2020912315

Paperback ISBN: 978-1-7351192-4-3
eBook ISBN: 978-1-7351192-5-0

Printed in the United States of America.

CONTENTS

Preface	ix
Resilient Reflections	1
God's Power	5
God's Awesomeness	7
The Father's Plan	9
New Beginnings	11
True Friend	15
Untold Story	17
Beautiful Names	21
Given Lemons	23
I Am	25
Servant of God	27
Daring to Look	29
Uniquely Made	31
Releasing the Hurt	33
Inhale, Exhale, Unveil	35
Rising High	37
Wise Woman	39
Showers of Blessings	41
Can You Hear Me?	43
I Am the Clay	45
Centered!	47
Loyalty Speaks	51
Godly Wisdom	53
Faithful Risks	57
Wise Counsel	59
Outburst of Courage	61
Conversations with God	63
The Knock	65
Disguised Angels	67

Aroma of Prayer	69
The Race	71
Imperfections	73
The Lonely Road	75
Perfect Love	77
Dazzled!	81
Do You Revere Me?	83
Did You Pray Today?	87
Majestic Key	89
Pray	91
Unclaimed Gifts	93
What is Your Prayer?	95
Be Awesome	97
The Fighter	99
Smile, Daughter	103
Farewell Mask	105
The Purpose	107
My Child	109
Rise and Shine	111
Given Moments	113
Menu for Success	115
Who Am I?	117
It's Not Enough	119
A Woman of God	121
A Man of God	125
Everyday People	127
I Believe	129
Peace Within	131
God's Blessings	133
Fear	135
Fires of Hell	137
Freedom of Choice	139
Given Power	141

Amazed!	143
Who Are You?	145
Breathe	147
Challenges	149
Look at You!	151
Men of Old	153
Life's Storms	157
Never Give Up	159
Greatness	161
I Am His	163
Be Still	165
Let it Go	167
Lifesaver	169
Talk to Your Heart	171
Stand Up!	173
Boomerang	175
True Success	177
The Flow	179
Greatness	181
Trusting God	183
Victim?	185
God Wants You!	187
Smile, Sisters	189
Are You Ready?	191
Love Me!	193
The Unnoticed	195
Wrong and Right	197
Child of God	199
Words, Words, Words	203
Change	205
The Right Time	207
Stay Focused	209
Praise the Lord!	211

Live Your Life!	215
Fearless Freedom	217
Rock the World	219
Last Breath	221
God's Promises	223
Answered Prayers	225
A Glimpse of Heaven	229
101 Enlightening Thoughts	233
The Enlightened Letter	239
The Resilient Closing	241
About the Author	243

PREFACE

Poetry expresses the deepest thoughts and feelings of our souls. It empowers us when seeking a goal, encourages us to stay in control, and enlightens us toward being made whole.

I've always been fascinated with poems. As a child, I would cut them from old books, magazines, and newspaper articles and paste them into my own special poem book.

When I got older, I began to write my own poems. I couldn't wait for special occasions like Christmas and birthdays to give them as gifts to my family and friends!

One day, I gave my friend Esther a poem. She was so delighted; she urged me to have it published in a Christian magazine. Although I was humbly honored, I decided to wait for the right moment. Amazingly, it arrived May 1, 2017, when I had written sixty poems to publish my first book, *Enlighten Your Life*.

Writing my first book was a laborious journey, but it was also an enjoyable experience. And I owe it all to the Heavenly Father, His Son Jesus, and the Holy Spirit for making my adventure a gratifying one.

Additionally, I am thankful to my wonderful family and good friends for their love and encouragement.

To the readers of *Enlighten Your Life,* I am grateful for their support and positive feedback. And it is with great pleasure and much humility I share some of their comments on Amazon with you.

"Jeannie's book is not only inspirational; it is an example of the passion she shows for Christ. We've used books to discuss Christian experiences and how we can have faith and hope as we continue our journey in this world. I love her poetry and willingness to share her thoughts on paper. I plan to buy her next book and will be an avid collector as she produces more!"

—Wayne and Carmen Jones

"This book was so powerful, a demonstration of inspirational expression. I love the fact that each chapter began with a quoted Bible verse followed by profound poetry. Awesome."

—Andrea J. Barnes

Although *Enlighten Your Life* works wonderfully as a motivational book, I wanted to have all my poems compiled into one volume; therefore, my third book, *Poems for Hungry Souls,* was conceived. My second book, *The Successful Journey of Prayer,* was published in March 2020.

The poems in this book were lovingly crafted to help you find winning solutions, overcome challenging situations, and guide you to firmly stand on God's unmovable foundation.

It is my earnest desire and my greatest hope that this thought-provoking book helps inspire, invigorate, and improve your life!

Poems for Hungry Souls addresses many of life's issues that can lead to worry, stress and fear; but if you "Trust in the LORD with all your heart, And lean not on your own understanding; In all your ways acknowledge Him, And He shall direct your paths" Proverbs 3:5-6.

And finally, to my publisher, BMcTALKS Press, I am thankful for the opportunity to have this book, *Poems for Hungry Souls,* published. Also, to the book editors and designers, I am grateful for their excellent work.

—Jeannie Colon

I will instruct you and teach you in the way you should go; I will guide you with My eye.

Psalm 32:8

RESILIENT REFLECTIONS

As she looked back on her life, she thought, *What a mess!* Then she said, "Isn't it funny the way life presents itself as roller coasters of sorrow and joy, sickness and health, failure, and success?"

And as that woman of God pondered on those things, she smiled with great confidence; because she knew that it was only through His mercy and grace, she had made it thus far.

The purposeful woman was determined to find true happiness. Therefore, she fearlessly embraced powerful faith, and boldly entered God's Marvelous Throne of Grace seeking His blessings.

She strongly believed that God was the only One who could fix her mess, relieve her stress, and heal her distress.

That determined woman was so elated with God's love and compassion; she addressed her duress with priceless prayers and countless poems of loveliness.

On her journey to self-awareness, the enlightened woman remarkably learned how to manifest bitterness into cheerfulness, selfishness into graciousness, and mercilessness into acts of forgiveness. And when she found the path that led to unmovable meekness, untouchable steadfastness, and unmerited greatness, she was amazed beyond words!

Moreover, when that grateful woman yielded to God's perfect gifts of righteousness, she learned how to prevail over the roller coasters of unmanageable sorrows, unexpected sicknesses, and unpredictable failures.

Therefore, with much humbleness, extreme delightfulness, and uncontrollable eagerness, you are invited to enjoy *Poems for Hungry Souls.* It will definitely permeate your life with perfect blessings of completeness.

*God has spoken once,
Twice I have heard this:
That power belongs to God.*

Psalm 62:11

GOD'S POWER

God's power and wisdom are truly magnificent.
Magnificent and flawless are His marvelous works.

Works of His creation are completely amazing,
Amazing, and beautiful, they resound in nature.

Nature He displays in spectacular abundance,
Abundance that is without boundaries or limits.

Limits and imperfections appear not in His power,
Power He exercises with mercy and kindness.

Kindness and compassion mark His generous love,
Love that is perfect, precious, and delightful.

Delightful and magnificent are His glorious gifts,
Gifts that remind us to praise Him forever.

Forever He is, the Holy and Powerful God,
God the Almighty, the Alpha, and the Omega.

You alone are the Lord;
You have made heaven,
The heaven of heavens, with all their host,
The earth and everything on it,
The seas and all that is in them,
And You preserve them all.
The host of heaven worships You.

Nehemiah 9:6

GOD'S AWESOMENESS

My God is so awesomely patient and powerful.
He made this world incomprehensibly wonderful.
His glorious work is vivid, bright, and colorful.
My God is so awesomely patient and powerful.

My God is so awesomely patient and good.
He gives me blessings that no one else could.
On His rock of promises, I have always stood.
My God is so awesomely patient and good.

My God is so awesomely patient and great.
His plans can be mysterious but are never late.
I trust in Him even when He teaches me to wait.
My God is so awesomely patient and great.

My God is so awesomely patient and loving.
Without Him, I would not be much of anything.
I am so thankful for His abundance in giving.
My God is so awesomely patient and loving.

My God is so awesomely patient and marvelous.
He has forgiven me and made me righteous.
I thank Him daily for His Precious Son Jesus.
My God is so awesomely patient and marvelous.

For I know the thoughts that I think toward you, says the Lord, thoughts of peace and not of evil, to give you a future and a hope.

Jeremiah 29:11

THE FATHER'S PLAN

God created you for a wholesome plan.
He chose you even before the world began.

He purchased you at an awesome price.
It was with the blood of Jesus Christ.

Will you obey and praise Him every day?
Because of Him, you can know the way.

Therefore be truthful, useful, and faithful.
As well as respectful, merciful, and grateful.

And if you ever feel bad, sad, or even mad,
You can go to Him because He is your dad.

*Through the Lord's mercies we are not consumed,
Because His compassions fail not.
²³ They are new every morning;
great is Your faithfulness. ²⁴ "The Lord is my portion," says my soul,
"Therefore I hope in Him!"*

Lamentations 3:22-24

NEW BEGINNINGS

You are possible, because nothing is impossible with God Almighty.
Wake up to God's divine truth and leave all ungodly ties in the past.
It's a new day; let go of failures, negativity, and be ready to be mighty.
Position yourself to receive God's blessings, to do your given task.

You are possible, improve yourself, and you will achieve excellence.
Do not be anxious for anything, pray and everything will turn out fine.
You must have powerful faith and take chances to make a difference.
This is your moment, your day, your season, and your perfect time.

You are possible, because the sinful doors of the past are closed.
Open the door to the future and welcome God's greatness in.
You are destined for perfection, so be ready to be transposed.
Dream, visualize, develop, grow, and change who you have been.

You are possible, the road to success is often paved with much pain.
Move from your comfort zone and use your God-given potential.
You must learn to dance in the storm and shine brightly in the rain.
Embrace new hopes, new goals, new dreams; they are very essential.

You are possible; when you fall, get up and pick up the pieces.
Rise and be very thankful for a life that is constantly mending.
Climb mountains, cross seas, and create delightful masterpieces.
Ablaze your story with an awesome, amazing, and abiding ending.

You are possible, because you can create a new chapter for your story.
Allow your journey to commence, though the path may be difficult.
Let go of suffering and sadness and cling to God and be merry.
Self-love, self-confidence, and self-actualization will be the result.

You are possible, with new blessings, choices, and undertakings.
Cheers to a new life, new adventure, new friends, and a new day.
Look forward to new courage, new joys, and new understandings.
Remove old life, old hurts, old past, and old enemies from the way.

You are possible, when you let go and allow challenges to begin.
Create new habits, new moments, new ideas, and important plans.
Stay focused on the Lord, His Word, His people, and never give in.
Never stop, do not quit, and always work diligently with your hands.

You are possible, you can approach your life with a new attitude.
You were created to honor and glorify God, that is the whole story.
And when you get weary, be strengthened by abundant gratitude.
Your painful struggle can be an awesome and delightful glory.

You are possible, because you can embrace a brand new day.
Are you excited to craft a productive new future for yourself?
Get ready to crush imperfections and be a godly vessel today.
Everything is possible, when you love God, neighbor, and self.

*The righteous should choose his friends carefully,
For the way of the wicked leads them astray.*

Proverbs 12:26

TRUE FRIEND

We have been true and loyal friends for many years,
Experiencing lots of laughter, great sorrow, and much tears.
We have shared many secrets that no one else has known.
And the strength of our beautiful friendship has only grown.

Dear friend, you have been there for me "through thick and thin."
Though we are different, sometimes it seems you are my twin.
You helped me without reproach, when I was tired and in pain.
Your support for me is always free of hidden motives or gain.

Girlfriend, I cannot stand it when we disagree, fuss, and fight.
But when we make up, it is refreshing, delightful, and right.
My buddy, you are a sweet angel sent from Heaven above.
I cherish our friendship and thank God for our pure love.

When I needed a shoulder to cry on, you showed me compassion.
You overlooked my imperfections with respect and not distraction.
I am overwhelmed by your empathy, support, and lovingkindness.
And I am thankful for your understanding, humor, and meekness.

I cannot imagine life without you, my good friend.
You are genuine, trustworthy, and truly a godsend.
My faithful pal, I hope our great friendship lasts forever,
And I pray that Heaven be our final and eternal endeavor.

And not only that, but we also glory in tribulations, knowing that tribulation produces perseverance; ⁴and perseverance, character; and character, hope. ⁵Now hope does not disappoint, because the love of God has been poured out in our hearts by the Holy Spirit who was given to us.

Romans 5:3-5

UNTOLD STORY

We all have a unique and untold story deep within.
It is a story concealed and settled under thick skin.
This special history penetrates deep into the soul.
It is a secret veiled and protected, never to extol.

These frightening narratives take hold in the mind,
Experiences we struggle with and have resigned.
It may be a tale of disappointment that tears us apart,
Which we then hide away at the bottom of the heart.

Yours may be the remnant of dreams that have been shattered
Or a memory that makes you feel naked, afraid, and battered.
We refuse to share these things for fear we will be rejected.
We believe we will be judged, disliked, and disrespected.

But in truth, each story is a beautiful hidden treasure.
They are not ours to keep, cover, or hide with displeasure.
We may think our stories are not valuable or worthwhile,
But someone may need to hear it to help restore their smile.

Some struggle with finances, spiritual issues, illness, or divorce,
The death of a loved one, poor choices, or something of that sort.
Therefore, we must make a great difference and never bury our voice.
But truly reach out to those who are hurting and make the right choice.

Do not worry about the critics, the arrogant, or disguised ones.
They also have unique stories hidden under their tongues.
Have great courage and share your delightful agonizing distress.
You might help someone today by relieving their heavy stress.

So, change the way you think and do not dwell on the past.
You can become an encourager and make your story last.
When you unmask your treasure, you help someone succeed
Because your story is an imprisoned jewel just waiting to be freed.

He who overcomes, I will make him a pillar in the temple of My God, and he shall go out no more. I will write on him the name of My God and the name of the city of My God, the New Jerusalem, which comes down out of heaven from My God. And I will write on him My new name.

Revelation 3:12

BEAUTIFUL NAMES

Holy Father, the Creator, Almighty God, YHWH is His name.
Jehovah, Righteous One, God of Abraham, Shepherd, Elohim.
Abba Father, Most High, Alpha and Omega, I AM, Still the Same.
Lord of Hosts, King of Glory, True God, and Supreme Being.

Jesus Christ, where Christ is not a surname but is Anointed One.
Emmanuel, Son of God, High Priest, Mediator, and True Light.
Redeemer, Master, Savior, Counselor, Rock, and Beloved Son.
Morning Star, Rabbi, the Word; He is also our power and might.

God, Holy Spirit, Witness, Teacher; His name we gladly proclaim.
Spirit of Holiness, Comforter, Spirit of Life, and Spirit of Freedom.
Eternal Spirit, Holy Ghost, Helper; He knows our sorrow and pain.
Intercessor, Revealer, Spirit of Truth, and Advocate of Wisdom.

Christians, the Church, Disciples of God, and Followers of Christ.
Brethren, Priests, God's Holy People; we are bought with a price.
The Bride of Jesus, the people who accepted His great sacrifice.
Elect Lady, Saints, Believers, Faithful; great names for the wise.

And we know that all things work together for good to those who love God, to those who are the called according to His purpose.

Romans 8:28

GIVEN LEMONS

They say, "When life gives you lemons, make sweet lemonade."
But what if your lemons are bitter and you are sourly dismayed?

When life gives you lemons, never be surprised or afraid.
Neither be rude, hateful, obnoxious, nor let others persuade.

When life gives you lemons, be smart and seek aid.
Find wisdom even if you have been brutally betrayed.

When life gives you lemons, do not close your heart or resist.
But open your soul to truth and kindness and you will persist.

When life gives you lemons, do not make a big parade.
Ask for something better like watermelon as an upgrade.

When life gives you lemons, do not be angry, resentful, or afraid.
But mix the lemon juice with honey, and you will have an accolade.

When life gives you lemons, do not hide behind a barricade.
Be confident and ferocious just like an unshackled renegade.

When life gives you lemons, you do not have to make lemonade.
Trust in the Lord with all your heart as you have always prayed.

*Delight yourself also in the Lord,
And He shall give you the desires of your heart.*

Psalm 37:4

I AM

I am happy to have an exciting life to live.
I am joyful to learn how to love and forgive.
I am peaceful enough to be freed from any stress.
I am satisfied because I no longer live in distress.

Gracious am I to have mercy, hope, and peace.
Powerful am I to be His awesome masterpiece.
Thankful am I to have knowledge and wisdom.
Sanctified am I to have a positively clear vision.

Grateful for my individuality and uniqueness, I am.
Delighted to receive His love and forgiveness, I am.
Confident to have understanding and freedom, I am.
Blessed to be a part of His perfect Kingdom, I am.

I am Your servant;
Give me understanding,
That I may know Your testimonies.

Psalm 119:125

SERVANT OF GOD

It is an honor to be called a servant of the True God.
What a blessing it is to serve the Most Powerful Lord!
It feels good to work for Him, in much delight and joy.
It is not in vain I serve Him; that is the truth I employ.

Powerful prayers have always been my support.
Salvation, service, and strength are all I can report.
I often ask Him for forgiveness, faith, and guidance.
And to bring His truth and love to my remembrance.

May I never forget fervent prayer is an effective tool.
And when tested, may I not act like a heathen or fool.
I understand that my Savior received anger and hate,
So I should not be dismayed if persecution is my fate.

Therefore, I ask the all-knowing God to always protect me,
And keep both my eyes turned to Him that I may clearly see.
I want to obey Him, fulfill my purpose, and finish my goal.
My plan is to love Him with all my mind, body, and soul.

*Your hands have made me and fashioned me;
Give me understanding, that I may learn Your commandments.
^{74}Those who fear You will be glad when they see me,
Because I have hoped in Your word.*

Psalm 119:73-74

DARING TO LOOK

Open your eyes and look in the mirror.
Come closer and you will see much clearer.
Dare to take a chance and fasten your eyes.
You might be in for a delightful surprise.

Do you see the twinkling and shining sparkle?
They are made in beauty; in excellence they dazzle.
Look at the reflection to the window of your soul.
That will be your best friend even when you are old.

Do not be afraid to stare into the looking glass.
Stop and gaze; do not always rush by when you pass.
God made you in His own image, didn't you know?
So love yourself, and do not act like you are the foe.

You were created in perfection, so be happy and grin.
Accept your uniqueness, stand tall and be ready to win.
Your true self is waiting to be valued and appreciated.
Open your eyes, enjoy who you are, and be invigorated!

I am dark, but lovely,
O daughters of Jerusalem.

Song of Solomon 1:5(a)

UNIQUELY MADE

Beautiful woman of dark mocha skin,
You shine and glow, deep from within.
Your perfectly luscious, thick-rounded lips
Speak gracefully of your voluptuous hips.

Your fine nose is shaped differently from most.
Of your soft kinky hair, you have reason to boast.
I can hear the truth spoken in your confident voice;
It speaks with wisdom, knowing it has a choice.

Lovely woman of dark-brown skin color,
Your fragrance smells sweet like a flower.
Girlfriend, no one compares to you by far.
You are magnificent just like a twinkling star.

Black woman, you are exquisitely made in uniqueness.
God created you in His awesome perfect and likeness.
Though some may look down on you, beautiful Ebony,
Never forget that you are lovely, flawless, and Heavenly.

Brethren, I do not count myself to have apprehended; but one thing I do, forgetting those things which are behind and reaching forward to those things which are ahead, ¹⁴ I press toward the goal for the prize of the upward call of God in Christ Jesus.

Philippians 3:13-14

RELEASING THE HURT

Disheartening, ugly, and undesiring hurt.
I blow you away just like worthless dirt.
I have locked the door and thrown away the key.
Because you no longer have hold or power over me.

I have an appointment with victory and success.
I want to be equipped to give them my absolute best.
Therefore, I will not think or even remember you.
Because you have given me much pain and sorrow too.

Hurt, I am saying goodbye because you no longer exist.
You have been removed from my mind and my wanted list.
But I will be forever grateful for your much-needed lesson.
You have truly taught me how to become a better person.

So I say goodbye old hurt, awful pain, and suffering.
You were very manipulating, puzzling, and smothering.
But through you I learned to love myself and became strong.
It is all because of you, hurt, that now I can sing a new song.

If indeed you have heard Him and have been taught by Him, as the truth is in Jesus: ²² that you put off, concerning your former conduct, the old man which grows corrupt according to the deceitful lusts, ²³ and be renewed in the spirit of your mind, ²⁴ and that you put on the new man which was created according to God, in true righteousness and holiness.

Ephesians 4:21-24

INHALE, EXHALE, UNVEIL

Vanity, rejection, and ignorance are unable to see her the same.
Stress, peer pressure, and arrogance cannot recognize her name.

Depression, chaos, and impatience no longer live at her location.
Jealousy, misery, and hate cannot stand her love and motivation.

Secrets, envy, and lies are desperately looking for protection.
Addiction, excuses, and drama are craving for her attention.

Insecurities, sadness, and anger are begging for her affection.
Worry, acceptance, and anxiety are in constant contention.

Unawareness, slothfulness, and doubt are seeking her admiration.
Pain, fear, and idleness are stubbornly waiting for a connection.

Slander, obsession, and abuse can no longer wait to prevail.
Because that woman has learned to inhale, exhale, and unveil.

"Have I not commanded you? Be strong and of good courage; do not be afraid, nor be dismayed, for the Lord your God is with you wherever you go."

Joshua 1:9

RISING HIGH

Are you planning on reaching the delightful blue sky?
Tell me the truth; how high do you think you can fly?
Do you want to be strong, successful, and limitless?
Then go for it, and do not settle for anything less!

Are you prepared to touch the beautiful sky?
There is so much abundance, and that is not a lie.
Victory can be yours in a moment at any time.
Dedicate yourself and always be ready to shine.

Are you ready to shoot to the infinite blue sky?
Do you really believe you can fly extremely high?
If you are determined, work hard, endure, you will thrive.
And you will attain your dreams and goals, the true prize.

She opens her mouth with wisdom,
And on her tongue is the law of kindness.

Proverbs 31:26

WISE WOMAN

When a woman of God knows she is beautifully made,
Her smile is lovely and genuine; it glows just like pure jade.
And she is never pretentious by wearing a hidden masquerade.
Because she shines brightly into the darkest part of any shade.

When a wise woman knows she was created to be beautiful,
She conducts herself with grace and makes herself useful.
When challenges come, she diligently prays and remain faithful.
Because she has truly learned the importance of being peaceful.

When a confident woman knows she was wonderfully created,
She allows the perfect love of God to be awesomely promulgated.
Her life will be brightly illuminated and exceptionally elevated.
Because she understands every day should be greatly celebrated.

When a smart woman knows she is valuable and more than just bait,
She wastes no time gossiping, complaining, or letting success wait.
She never relies on others' validation but appreciates her worthiness.
And she pursues her goals and dreams with passion and eagerness.

I will make them and the places all around My hill a blessing; and I will cause showers to come down in their season; there shall be showers of blessing.

Ezekiel 34:26

SHOWERS OF BLESSINGS

Showers of blessings, please fall on us abundantly today.
Wash over us with your water, that we may never go astray.

Showers of blessings, we hear the outpouring of your voice.
The holy raindrops soak us like there is no other choice.

Showers of blessings, pour on us a deluge of protection.
Purify us with outbursts of love, faith, and compassion.

Showers of blessings, never cease quenching our soul.
Without your sweet river, our life cannot be made whole.

Showers of blessings, can you hear the torrent call?
Clean our violent thoughts that we may never fall.

Showers of blessings, drench us with confidence and peace.
Rain on us forever, so we bear precious fruits that never cease.

*"It shall come to pass
That before they call, I will answer;
And while they are still speaking, I will hear."*

Isaiah 65:24

CAN YOU HEAR ME?

Lord, can You hear me desperately calling to You?
I am so incredibly stressed, depressed, and have no rest.
My tears are flowing, and I do not know what to do.
I am crying, sighing, and discouraged from this test.

Lord, I ask for Your mercy; will You show me You care?
I am imploring, outpouring, humbly asking, and appealing.
Father, I long for Your mercy and grace; please come near.
I am kneeling, pleading, and longing for Your perfect healing.

Lord, I am despairingly praying, do You recognize my voice?
I am groping, hoping, and exploding, I need Your help coping.
Father, please answer my plea; You are my only true choice.
Do not leave me in the pits, I beg You through my sad moping.

Lord, hear me, I am faithfully and lovingly reaching out to You.
I am seeking Your favor; will You listen to the words I say?
Please give me blessings of peace, wisdom, and forgiveness too.
I want my life to truly glorify You, each and every single day.

But now, O Lord,
You are our Father;
We are the clay, and You our potter;
And all we are the work of Your hand.

Isaiah 64:8

I AM THE CLAY

Father, I am the clay and You are the Perfect Potter.
Mold me and make me into Your delightful daughter.
Purify my heart and make it clean like crystal water.
Lift my feet to walk lightly without a heavy fetter.

Transform my mind to follow Your perfect Word each day.
Form my lips into a vessel to praise You in all that I say.
Shape my eyes to see the beauty of Your marvelous way.
And keep my soul focused, that I may never go astray.

Lord, perfect my life that I may refrain from secret sin.
Chisel away all bitterness, anger, and pain from within.
Renew my imperfect broken spirit and make it whole again.
Your joy, peace, truth, and love, I seek to sweetly drink in.

Cut away my arrogance, evil thoughts, hate, and vexation.
Carve my heart into an element of love and compassion.
Father shape my wayward feet to follow your direction.
Model my life to be a masterpiece after Jesus's perfection.

For we walk by faith, not by sight.

2 Corinthians 5:7

CENTERED!

Center me, O Lord, and place me in the palm of Your hand.
Empower me and make my life pure, humble, and grand.

Search me, O Lord, and recover me from the wicked.
Open the eyes of my soul that Your name be lifted.

Build me up, O Lord, and shower me with much compassion.
Illuminate my life with truth to be called Your possession.

Bless me with sweet victory, O Lord, that I may truly rise above.
Cover me with courage, that I may dwell in Your perfect love.

Guide me in the right way that I may arrive to my final destination.
Teach me life's purpose that I may safely dwell in Your habitation.

Place me in the midst of challenges, O Lord, that I may become strong.
Transform me into Your perfect vessel to distinguish right from wrong.

Clothe me with serenity, O Lord, that I may hear Your caring voice.
Extinguish my fears and give me boldness to make the right choice.

Change me, O Lord, to accept Your truth and perfect righteousness.
Remove from me the ordinary and replace it with Your perfectness.

Embrace me with your gift of love, Your Precious Son Jesus.
Introduce me to His marvelous way, that I may be cautious.

Align me, O Lord, with the power of Your perfect word.
Let Your teachings be not silenced but be clearly heard.

Help me to change the world, O Lord, by praising Your name.
I am thankful for Your precious Word that I can now proclaim.

Grant me opportunities with boldness, O Lord, to glorify You.
I desire to be faithful, loyal, and successful in everything I do.

Change me, O Lord, and help me become who I was created to be.
Furnish me with great compassion and true love to be like Thee.

Rescue me from the wicked, O Lord, and give me wisdom.
I want Your deliverance, courage, and unmatched freedom.

Remove addictions from me, O Lord, and give me good health.
Destroy my lack, wants, and poverty and give me Your wealth.

Bestow on me spiritual blessings, O Lord, to abide in Your ways.
Unshackle me from the bondage of sin and enlighten my days.

Open doors of solutions for me, O Lord, that I may be victorious.
Anoint me with Your love, power, and tenacity to be laborious.

Release me from past failures, O Lord, and also unrepented woe.
Show me how to run life's race with endurance, that I may grow.

Enhance my life, O Lord, that I may obey Your blessed commands.
Provide me with perfect wisdom when I hold Your powerful hands.

Create in me a clean heart, O Lord, and help me to become like You.
Center me that I may stand firmly and unmovable in all that is true.

*He who follows righteousness and mercy
finds life, righteousness, and honor.*

Proverbs 21:21

LOYALTY SPEAKS

Hello, my name is Loyalty; when I speak, Honesty listens.
My dear friends are Mr. Faithfulness and Ms. Truthfulness.

I have always devoted my full allegiance to my friends.
I adhere to all my commitments, promises, and goals.

I will never leave you, abandon you, or even disappoint you.
And I promise to be reliable, dependable, and delightful too.

When you call out for me, I will always be of good cheer.
I will lavish you with compassion, consistency, and truth.

I hate deception, cheating, lies, unfaithfulness, and dishonesty.
Trust me, I am not entertained with foolish or deceitful games.

I am in love with integrity, sincerity, morality, and devotion.
My faithful friend is karma, and we have a great relationship.

Therefore, when you call my name, be very trusting and respectful.
Never confuse me with Mrs. Trickery, Mr. Fool, or Ms. Drama.

*Happy is the man who finds wisdom,
And the man who gains understanding;*
*¹⁴For her proceeds are better than the profits of silver,
And her gain than fine gold.*

Proverbs 3:13-14

GODLY WISDOM

Godly wisdom, O Godly wisdom.
I am told you are more valuable than silver and gold.
And you are also perfect, awesome, loving, and bold.

Godly wisdom, O Godly wisdom.
You are dressed in gracefulness, generosity, and kindness.
And you are adorned with honesty, purity, and truthfulness.

Godly wisdom, O Godly wisdom.
Teach me your ways that I may have much understanding.
And show me how to be holy, confident, and outstanding.

Godly wisdom, O Godly wisdom.
I know you are gentle, compassionate, and peaceful.
Help me be calm, disciplined, sensible, and useful.

Godly wisdom, O Godly wisdom.
You display honor, glory, prudence, and impartiality.
And you illuminate me with humility, faith, and sincerity.

Godly wisdom, O Godly wisdom.
Be my supplier, advisor, motivator, and provider.
And give me the desire to successfully reach higher.

Godly wisdom, O Godly wisdom.
Instruct me how to refrain from bitterness, envy, and arrogance.
And guide me to overcome selfishness, anger, and ignorance.

Godly wisdom, O Godly wisdom.
Rid me of dishonesty, lies, chaos, and ungodly pleasure.
And edify me to receive your most divine and valued treasure.

Godly wisdom, O Godly wisdom.
Free me from evil strife, immaturity, sadness, and any confusion.
And erase from me hatred, discrimination, and selfish ambition.

Godly wisdom, O Godly wisdom.
Bless me to walk circumspectly in your power, grace, and honor.
Equip me with knowledge and understanding, every minute and hour.

By faith Abraham obeyed when he was called to go out to the place which he would receive as an inheritance. And he went out, not knowing where he was going.

Hebrews 11:8

FAITHFUL RISKS

Excellent rewards cannot be attained without taking any risk.
You have to be extremely brave and do not look for a quick fix.
Stay alert to recognize God's gifts and His winning chances,
And be ready to jump in after taking the required glances.

Do not allow fear to stop you from what you want to attain.
True success cannot be embraced without feeling any pain.
Realize some battles you will lose, and others you will win.
However, you will never know until you learn to leap in.

Taking risks can improve, change, and better your life.
When you exercise great faith, you become exceedingly wise.
Visualize obtaining extraordinary and extravagant awards.
When you take risks, you will receive amazing rewards.

Learn to be daring, brave, and embrace important risks.
Never waste your time by delaying or playing silly tricks.
And you will be recompensed with goodness and confidence.
Remember, bravery and risks can produce glorious opulence.

*Listen to counsel and receive instruction,
That you may be wise in your latter days.*

Proverbs 19:20

WISE COUNSEL

Friends: adhere to wise counsel, and do not reject good advice.
Accept the instruction of the prudent and learn to rationalize.

When pursuing wisdom, remember knowledge is great wealth.
Know that understanding is beneficial to your spiritual health.

The decisions you make today will affect tomorrow's vision.
Where there is no self-control, God's people fall from wisdom.

A wise person listens and follows proper guidance and direction.
But a foolish person despises good teachings and also correction.

Nothing can truly compare with the persuasion of the wise.
They are truly a blessing of joy and peace to the human eyes.

Good counsel is like a tree, providing nourishing fruits to the soul.
It is more valuable than any jewelry made of pure silver or gold.

Only fools despise wisdom that gives freedom and conviction.
But the wise diligently seek, accept, and embrace its perfection.

"Be strong and of good courage, do not fear nor be afraid of them; for the LORD your God, He is the One who goes with you. He will not leave you nor forsake you."

Deuteronomy 31:6

OUTBURST OF COURAGE

A sudden deluge of hardship, adversity, fear, and devastation,
But we are covered by faith, confidence, and determination.

When life attacks us with undesired surprises and fearful moments,
We should never allow them to tear us apart or leave us with aliments.

When we accept, cultivate, and declare outbursts of courage,
We become wise, mature, confident, and without any rage.

When we face unlawful demands or risk becoming unfaithful,
May we cultivate endurance and diligence to stay prayerful.

If we put on the full and mighty armor of God and be courageous,
We will successfully fight the foe with the power of God within us.

*He said, "Please, show me Your glory." *¹⁹*Then He said, "I will make all My goodness pass before you, and I will proclaim the name of the* LORD *before you. I will be gracious to whom I will be gracious, and I will have compassion on whom I will have compassion." *²⁰*But He said, "You cannot see My face; for no man shall see Me, and live."*

Exodus 33:18-20

CONVERSATIONS WITH GOD

Almighty God, if I could only see Your face and not die,
I would be so awesomely happy, I would not even cry.

Heavenly Father, if I could touch Your powerful hand,
I would hold on tight, and I would feel awesomely grand.

Lord, if I could hear Your loving and patient voice,
I would not be afraid, I would continuously rejoice.

Abba Father, if I could just hug Your marvelous feet,
I would feel protected, peaceful, and delightfully complete.

Loving God, if I could see Your pure and Holy smile,
I would be illuminated and enlightened for a good while.

Holy Father, if You would walk with me every day,
I would tell You all my troubles and ask You to stay.

Great God, if I could hold You now and not wait for the future,
I would be transformed into a brand new and perfect creature.

Behold, I stand at the door and knock. If anyone hears My voice and opens the door, I will come in to him and dine with him, and he with Me.

Revelation 3:20

27

THE KNOCK

Hello, can you hear me knocking at your door?
Please, heed to the tap, and do not hide and ignore.

You say, "Who is there?" as though you cannot see.
And you securely lock the door and hide away the key.

I am pleading with you, please let me come inside.
I will teach you how to be faithful and how to abide.

I will whisper to you in a tender and loving voice.
And when you understand, you will truly rejoice.

"Who is there?" you loudly and angrily ask again.
"Will you please go? I don't recognize your name."

You turn me away and say, "No solicitation."
Why do you decline your chance at salvation?

It is sad to know you refuse the opportunity of a lifetime.
And you have willfully rejected the Lord, one more time!

Do not forget to entertain strangers, for by so doing some have unwittingly entertained angels.

Hebrews 13:2

DISGUISED ANGELS

The true purpose of life is to be kind to everyone you meet.
Angels may appear as strangers, so stay extremely sweet.

Adopt a spirit of goodness, kindness, and inspiration.
Give the people you encounter the gift of true motivation.

Earthly blessings are given to share, enjoy, and delight.
But Heavenly treasures are wonderful and out of sight.

Use charity to assist those who lack or are in need.
And bless those who seek your help and good deed.

God asks you to shine bright in this dark and evil world.
Never be weary or fearful, but be compassionate and bold.

Always be ready to impart the Good News to a stranger.
That means Jesus's death, and going way back to His manger.

Ask God for His help to be strong, wise, faithful, and mature.
You will discern good from evil and be strengthened and endure.

So remember to be friendly and warmhearted to everyone you meet.
They may be God's disguised angels, sent to help make you complete.

Let my prayer be set before You as incense.

Psalm 141:2(a)

AROMA OF PRAYER

Prayer is a sweet-smelling aroma of a true and faithful soul.
It is a redolence of myrrh to the Lord and it makes us whole.

Prayer is like the scent of all the world's costliest spices.
Its smell becomes more magnificent as its beauty rises.

Prayer is like the awesome savor of delicious food.
It generates a tantalizing fragrance of all that is good.

Prayer is the pure essence of a delightful peace offering.
Its aura is like the perfume of a beautiful garden flowering.

Prayer is the Spirit's anointing fragrance of perfect peace.
Its atmosphere of love, joy, and wisdom can never cease.

Prayer is like the overflowing incense of an obedient heart.
When it reaches the Heavenly Father, it truly sets us apart.

Do you not know that those who run in a race all run, but one receives the prize? Run in such a way that you may obtain it.

1 Corinthians 9:24

THE RACE

I am fully equipped and ready to run the spiritual race.
I asked the Almighty God to please give me His grace.

I will successfully begin my difficult journey today.
I have trained for every minute in every single way.

My goal is to proceed with wisdom, strength, and stamina.
I will soar like a falcon and run like a cheetah in Africa.

I will resist Satan's darts while holding on to God's shield.
Nothing will stop me; not even to worldly treasures I will yield.

I may get tired, frustrated, and tempted, but I will not give up.
The Alpha and Omega awaits me, so I have no time to stop.

I will not slow down nor deviate, but I will run extremely fast.
I will be diligent and faithful as I stay on the righteous path.

Heaven is my goal and destination; I cannot wait to get my crown.
So I will run steady with perseverance, until the race is all done.

Jesus's blood provides me with all the strength and energy I need.
I am confident I will win the difficult race if I stay at the right speed.

The journey may be bumpy and rough, but I am confident I will win.
I will claim the delightful victory because I have been freed from sin.

I can imagine God saying, "Well done, my precious child, come in."
And Jesus and the Holy Spirit showing their pride with a grin.

But the Lord said to Samuel, "Do not look at his appearance or at his physical stature, because I have refused him. For the Lord does not see as man sees; for man looks at the outward appearance, but the Lord looks at the heart."

1 Samuel 16:7(b)

IMPERFECTIONS

Beautiful imperfections, you are a benefit in disguise.
A lovely impairment, I see you and I honestly recognize.
You are always remarkable, authentic, and incredibly wise.
And you are a blessing under God's perfect watchful eyes.

Physical imperfections, you are unique and so splendid.
You are a special material that does not need to be mended.
You always keep me focused; I feel loved and attended.
And I will fervently pray on knees that are joyfully bended.

Lovely imperfections, guide me to have my life rearrange.
You have made a woman of me, and that I will never exchange.
Thank you for helping me rise above and into the next range.
You have taught me to be humble, and that I will not change.

Lord, thank You for my imperfections, and may I firmly take a stand.
I do not want to be mediocre, what I desire is to be awesomely grand.
Give me knowledge and wisdom to obey Your blessed command.
I will embrace my imperfections, although I may not fully understand.

Narrow is the gate and difficult is the way which leads to life, and there are few who find it.

Matthew 7:14(b)

THE LONELY ROAD

There is an untold story of a very dark and lonely road.
You may not want to hear it, if you are carrying a load.

The solitary road was a winding one with a difficult turn.
It can be upsetting to the mind and make the stomach churn.

Its gloominess can drive anyone to sadness, madness, or despair.
And its isolation can leave your spirit and soul feeling very bare.

If you travel it at night, you might feel detached and alone.
But over time, its utter quiet can make you feel at home.

That lonesome road can help you build character and courage.
If you stay on its track, you will become strong and also manage.

So never avoid traveling that dark, perilous, and dreary road.
There you will find needed lessons, to help you carry life's load.

For God so loved the world that He gave His only begotten Son, that whoever believes in Him should not perish but have everlasting life.

John 3:16

PERFECT LOVE

Why did You leave Your home of perfection and glory?
Why did You give us so much abundance and victory?
Why did You come to this world of evil and darkness?
Why do You care about the ungrateful, Your Highness?

You healed the sick, raised the dead, and gave the blind sight.
They were envious of Your popularity, purity, and great might.
Why couldn't they comprehend You wanted to be their friend?
All You ask for is obedience, and their souls You would mend.

Savior, You gently said, "Let the little children come to me."
I believe the Kingdom of Heaven has many of them to see.
You gave Your love and compassion unsparingly to the poor.
And You cried bitterly when they died, were oppressed, and sore.

The evildoers disrespected Your Father's temple, His Holy House.
It was used for all sorts of things: like gambling and a farmhouse.
You detested the things they taught because they were not true.
So they counted You as an enemy and decided to get rid of You.

You cried tears of blood, but You obeyed Your Father's will.
Son of God, You were the only One who could that plan fulfill.
You glorified Your Father and brought Him to remembrance.
Though You had no worldly riches, You lived in much abundance.

The liars and ungodly accused You of many things You did not do.
They refused to accept Your great love, wisdom, and compassion too.
They brought false witnesses against You, but to them You submitted.
Lord, You carried the heavy cross because You were deeply committed.

They hammered Your hands and feet in rebellion and with slander.
I cannot imagine why they pounded Your flesh with so much anger!
The blood that dripped from Your body, no one could control it.
But the horrible pain and anguish You felt did not destroy Your spirit.

You could have called thousands of angels to fight for You.
But You remained silent and allowed them to mock You too.
Your love, perfection, and mercy, they could not understand.
They wanted to shame You, and they demanded it beforehand.

You said, "Father, forgive them, for they don't know what they do."
How could You love them when they were hurting and killing You?
And the one who sold You for a few silver coins did not obey the rules.
They all missed such a chance at life with You, those deceitful fools!

Why didn't You speak up and defend Your holiness and innocence?
Why did You let them accuse You of lies and undeniable nonsense?
Why did You allow to be charged of things like disrupted behavior?
Why couldn't they understand You are Christ, the Lord and Savior?

They hatefully accused You of doing unproven and lawless things.
And said You proclaimed to be the Lord of lords and King of kings.
They mocked and provoked You, even as You took your last breath.
You suffered a horrible, torturous, and excruciating, undeserving death.

They assumed the battle was won and You were brutally defeated.
But it was just the beginning because love can never be depleted.
In agony, You cried, "Father, into Your hands I commit my spirit!"
Then the contract was sealed when You lastly said, "It is finished."

And in just three days, You rose victoriously from the dead.
Your disciples quickly remembered all the things You had said.
When You appeared to Your followers, they were surprised.
Until that day they did not understand, You are the true Christ.

You promised to send the Comforter to help them do Your work.
They needed assistance to successfully continue God's handiwork.
When You were ready to go, You said goodbye to your friends.
And as You were leaving, they saw You to the clouds ascend.

"Son of God, please tell me why You did it?" I curiously ask.
"Why did You leave your home in glory to take up such a task?
Jesus Christ, why did You voluntarily suffer and painfully die?"
I cannot comprehend Your great sacrifice, so I ponder, and I cry.

Your perfect love is simply awesome, amazing, and contagious.
It is greatly infectious, delightful, loyal, and always unpretentious.
Thank you for being kind, patient, peaceful, and long-suffering.
And for paying salvation's price with Your sacrificial offering.

Why do You love us? We are not worthy of Your love and compassion.
We are wretched, unfit, and sinful; help us to show You appreciation.
Teach us to be like You, that our feet may always wander from evil.
Make us strong and wise enough to conquer all schemes of the devil.

We have lived sinful lives of disobedience and much bitterness.
Continue to show us Your mercy, grace, love, and forgiveness.
We can never repay You for Your perfect compassion and sacrifice.
So we hope our obedience to Your awesome Word will truly suffice.

They looked to Him and were radiant,
And their faces were not ashamed.

Psalm 34:5

DAZZLED!

O splendorous shooting sparkle from within.
You used to shine and glitter all over my skin.

Priceless, irresistible, bright, and powerful gleam.
Your radiance would embrace me like the sunbeam.

You have hidden Your delightful light and left me in the dark.
Why aren't You showing me Your beautiful shining spark?

Wonderful, illuminating, God's Marvelous Light,
Reveal Your splendorous presence and dazzling sight.

I will not settle for the flicker of rhinestones or sequins.
What I desire is costly diamonds befitting for great queens.

Dazzling, sparkling, crystal-clear, and radiant jewel,
Your luminosity is warm and kind, never cold or cruel.

Bring back the gleam, the Light of brilliant flashing elegance.
I need Your brightness, Your guidance, and Your presence.

Then a voice came from the throne, saying, "Praise our God, all you His servants and those who fear Him, both small and great!"

Revelation 19:5

DO YOU REVERE ME?

My child, do you really know who I am?
Do you understand I am the Great I AM?

The Most Sovereign King, the One who made you.
I deserve to be loved, obeyed, and respected too.

When you speak and refer to My Holy Name,
Why do you use it in disrespect and in vain?

I sent My Only Son from Heaven to die for you.
I have given you the ultimate love and sacrifice too.

I have known you before you were in your mother's womb.
I created this earth for you to delightfully grow and bloom.

I have given you the perfect love that is priceless.
Did you know I created you in My own likeness?

Why don't you show appreciation and thank Me?
Did you forget I am not blind, but I can see?

You approach Me, your Heavenly Father, and demand.
Understand I am a king, the Most Powerful and Grand!

I can make you rise, and I can also make you fall.
I am the Heavenly Father who created you and all.

And when you are in trouble, you come to Me,
Expecting Me to answer you and set you free?

I take away your sorrow, when you are sad and blue.
And when you weep, I am very compassionate too.

When you lack, I abundantly bless you.
Do you realize all the things that I do?

I healed you when you were terribly sick.
I am close by when you are afflicted and weak.

My child, please reevaluate your life now.
And renew your mind; I will teach you how.

I am the Mighty King, and I abundantly give.
Why don't you learn from Me and also forgive?

I am the Compassionate and Generous Father.
Why are you not kind to your sister and brother?

I am God, the Almighty, the beginning and the end.
The Greatest of All, the One you do not want to offend.

So, My dear child, when you approach My Marvelous Throne,
Remember, I AM the Greatest and Most Powerful ever known!

—Almighty God

*My voice You shall hear in the morning, O Lord;
In the morning I will direct it to You,
And I will look up.*

Psalm 5:3

DID YOU PRAY TODAY?

When you woke up this morning, did you pray?
Did you thank God for giving you a brand new day?
Did you offer Him a prayer of thanksgiving?
For being alive, well, and still breathing?

When you opened your eyes, did you pray?
Were you grateful for your vision to see this new day?
Did you express your appreciation for His kindness?
And for His perfect love that is awesome and timeless?

When you placed your feet on the ground, did you pray?
Did you glorify Him for legs that can walk the right way?
Did you humbly remember your patient and Loving Creator?
And ask Him to help you magnify and mimic His behavior?

When you woke up this morning, did you thank the Lord?
Did you exalt the Sovereign King, the Mighty and Powerful God?
Were you grateful for your awakening and undeserving moment?
And for your loving family, friends, and even ruthless opponent?

When you woke up this morning, did you think about the Almighty?
Or did you start your day thanklessly, unappreciative, and unwisely?
He requires you to live a life pleasing and acceptable every day.
So be diligent, consistent, thankful, and remember to always pray.

The key of the house of David
I will lay on his shoulder;
So he shall open, and no one shall shut;
And he shall shut, and no one shall open.

Isaiah 22:22

MAJESTIC KEY

Marvelous key that opens God's Great Throne.
You are always with me, and I am never alone.

My perfect, undeserving, and awesome gift.
Stay with me forever, and do not ever drift.

You are a true privilege, an earnest devotion.
An endless driving power always in motion.

You bless me with victory and success.
Although I do not always pass the test.

You do what some people say is impossible.
Everything you do is good, true, and possible.

You have changed my darkest moments into pure light.
And You have replaced my weakness into great might.

Sweet loving prayer, I am happy you are my friend.
You are a blessing in disguise, a delightful godsend.

Please stay with me, O marvelous prayer and majestic key.
And help me become the person who God created me to be.

Pray without ceasing.

1 Thessalonians 5:17

38

PRAY

Pray in the morning.
Pray in the evening.

Pray in good times.
Pray in tough times.

Pray when you are glad.
Pray when life is hard.

Pray when you are tired.
Pray when it is required.

Pray when you are sad.
Pray when you are mad.

Pray for strength and power.
Pray every day and every hour.

Pray to have heavenly wisdom.
Pray diligently for God's Kingdom.

You ask and do not receive, because you ask amiss, that you may spend it on your pleasures.

James 4:3

UNCLAIMED GIFTS

Generous God, I don't want to miss Your delightful gifts.
I cry, but You do not see my tear.

I call, demand, and arrogantly ask,
Why don't You seem to do the task?

Lord, why are You hiding and ignoring me?
Please, answer my plea, while I am on my knee.

You said to only ask, and I will truly receive.
But I was unfaithful, and I did not believe.

When I prayed, I asked only for my family and self.
I forgot prayer is for everyone needing Your help.

You have given me great blessings in abundance.
Why aren't You showing me direction or guidance?

I have been disobedient, unfaithful, and also unkind.
Lord, forgive me and purify me with a renewed mind.

Father, I repent and implore Your gifts of righteousness.
I desire your marvelous love and wonderful graciousness.

Father, I do not want to ever miss Your delightful gifts.
And to regretfully be on Your Unclaimed Prayer List.

It is the list of unanswered prayers that were missed.
Because they were unacceptable and were dismissed.

Now this is the confidence that we have in Him, that if we ask anything according to His will, He hears us. ¹⁵ *And if we know that He hears us, whatever we ask, we know that we have the petitions that we have asked of Him.*

1 John 5:14-15

WHAT IS YOUR PRAYER?

What will your prayer be, O child of God?
What will you say that is different from the odd?

Do you want a pure and disciplined mind?
A character that is powerful, gentle, and kind?

What will your prayer be, O child of God?
What will you say that is delightful and awed?

You can ask Him to greatly broaden your vocation.
And to be refrained from sin, fear, and temptation.

What will your prayer be, O child of God?
What will you say without needing someone to applaud?

You must have powerful faith and wisdom to believe.
Know your prayers are being answered, and you will receive.

Let each of you look out not only for his own interests, but also for the interests of others.

Phillippians 2:4

BE AWESOME

Are you ready to believe?
Are you ready to receive?

Are you ready to forgive?
Are you ready to live?

Are you ready to know?
Are you ready to grow?

Are you ready for guidance?
Are you ready for abundance?

Are you truly ready to love?
Are you ready to rise above?

Are you ready to be useful?
Are you ready to be joyful?

Are you ready to no longer wait?
Are you ready to be awesomely great?

Fight the good fight of faith, lay hold on eternal life, to which you were also called and have confessed the good confession in the presence of many witnesses.

1 Timothy 6:12

THE FIGHTER

I knew a delightful girl who was a brave fighter.
She would make her walk and path much brighter.
This incredible sister was so awesomely tough.
But she was told, "You are not good enough."

I really enjoyed seeing her fighting spirit.
Her light and her passion were always in it.
And whenever she would kneel in prayer,
Her heart would sparkle with honesty and flair.

She had a wonderful strength I admired.
And when she used it, I would get inspired.
I loved to see her bright flame and burning fire.
It was so sad to know it would quickly expire.

One day, she lost all of her burning passion.
Because she was told it was not in fashion.
Where were her loyalty and utter devotion?
She buried it deep in a mysterious ocean.

They asked her to silence her wise voice.
And she did so without making a choice.
I was surprised to see she even authorized
The things she did not want compromised.

She was different from all the rest.
I always thought she would pass the test.
Instead, she allowed her dreams to be sold.
Because she was judged by all, young and old.

They even said she was lacking and poor
Although she aspired to have much more.
They mocked her and said, "You are not pretty."
And that was when she began to have self-pity.

Where are you now, my amazing conqueror?
Rise up and use your God-given power.
Please tell me where you can be found.
Blessed and beautiful woman renowned.

Will someone help me find her, to build her up?
I desperately want to ask her, "What's up?"
And I want to see her doing much better.
Because I miss that delightful go-getter!

*If I say, 'I will forget my complaint,
I will put off my sad face and wear a smile*

Job 9:27

SMILE, DAUGHTER

Smile, daughter, smile.
You are a genius, a star of royalty indeed.
And your heritage is of a wonderful breed.
You are made to please God; I hope you know.
So live your life rightly, and always to Him go.

Smile, daughter, smile.
Uniquely and confident you were created to be.
And when you open your eyes, you will clearly see.
Ignore all the critics, you will be wise if you believe.
Have faith in the Lord, and you will always achieve.

Smile, daughter, smile.
Be truthful, optimistic, and visualize your life.
And you will not have to worry about any strife.
Always take your time and frequently pray.
If you abide in the truth, you will please God every day.

Smile, daughter, smile.
Ask your Heavenly Father, He has an answer for you.
He will give you the sky, and all in it too.
So receive all your blessings and know you are a star.
Let your light shine brightly, to be seen extremely far.

Smile, daughter, smile.
Please love, respect, and be good to yourself.
And never forget, your dreams are your wealth.
If you hold on to your faith and trust in the Lord,
He will give you many blessings, instead of the rod.
So smile, daughter, smile!

Knowing this, that our old man was crucified with Him, that the body of sin might be done away with, that we should no longer be slaves of sin.

Romans 6:6

FAREWELL MASK

Goodbye, unfaithful and untruthful masquerade mask.
Keeping up with you and the Joneses was a great task.

Full of drama and fakeness, my life was truly a mess.
I lost reality, my identity, true friends, and even success.

All I gained was worry, hate, insecurities, and disgrace.
So I am disowning you and taking back my God-given face.

Goodbye, masquerade mask, social circle, and status quo.
I am content, confident, blessed, and loved, didn't you know?

Sorry I cannot even say, "see you later," or "until next time."
You have sucked the life from me and did not give me a dime.

But I will say, farewell, ciao, adios, cheerio, sayonara, and aloha.
Bye-bye, I am burying you down in the dirt; au revoir and ta-ta!

*"Everyone who is called by My name,
Whom I have created for My glory;
I have formed him, yes, I have made him."*

Isaiah 43:7

THE PURPOSE

Were you born to be sorrowful?
Or were you born to be joyful?

Were you born to be unskillful?
Or were you born to be useful?

Were you born to be forceful?
Or were you born to be peaceful?

Were you born to be doubtful?
Or were you born to be faithful?

Were you born to be just bored?
Or were you born to praise God?

I will praise You, for I am fearfully and wonderfully made;
Marvelous are Your works,
And that my soul knows very well.

Psalm 139:14

MY CHILD

My child, you were delightfully and wonderfully made.
In My image, you were perfectly and beautifully arrayed.
And when I lovingly formed you in your mother's womb,
It was for you to purposefully sparkle, shine, and bloom.

My wonderful child, you are the apple of My eyes.
I made you so lovely, please do not wear a disguise.
My love for you is intense and deep as the ocean.
I will help you prosper, whenever you are in motion.

My precious child, let Me show you the right way.
Do not listen to the negative things that people say.
If you obey My commands, I will bless your soul.
And I will open doors for you to achieve your goal.

My brave child, I see the fearless look in your eyes.
I am the One who put it there, and it is not a surprise.
Therefore, never give up when you have difficult days.
I will be your supporter when you abide in My ways.

My blessed child, you have nothing to fight for nor to defend.
I have given you a home, and a great future to ascend.
Know you are My creation, My offspring, and My friend.
And I will be here for you, from the beginning to the end.

—God

This is the day the Lord has made;
We will rejoice and be glad in it.

Psalm 118:24

RISE AND SHINE

This is the day that the Lord has made.
I will be happy to rise and shine.

My eyes are opened, and my feet can move.
I am so blessed I can rise and shine.

I have planned my day and without delay.
I need the strength to rise and shine.

There is no time to waste, I must go in haste.
I am now ready to rise and shine.

Today is a gift, so I will never drift.
Now is the time to rise and shine.

This is the day that the Lord has made.
Please, help me, Lord, to rise and shine!

But do not forget to do good and to share, for with such sacrifices God is well pleased.

Hebrews 13:16

GIVEN MOMENTS

If I can help an afflicted child,
I shall not live in vain.

If I can make time for a stranger,
I shall not live in vain.

If I can give love and compassion,
I shall not live in vain.

If I can save an innocent life,
I shall not live in vain.

If I can make a difference in the world,
I shall not live in vain.

If I can seize a God-given moment,
I shall not live in vain.

Do not be overcome by evil, but overcome evil with good.

Romans 12:21

MENU FOR SUCCESS

I am extremely hungry for success.
Will someone help satisfy my need to progress?

The menu is balanced to help change my state.
I will eat everything that you put on my plate.

The breakfast you serve me is delicious pain.
I am eating all of it, and I do not complain.

The lunch you have prepared is yummy hate.
Please put a lot of it all over my plate.

Am I having disappointments for dinner?
They will help make me a high-spirited winner!

I want scrumptious negativity as a snack.
Will you wrap it all up and pile it in a stack?

I am thirsty for some delectable criticism.
Pour every drop of it into my cup of optimism.

I am extremely hungry for success.
Will someone help satisfy my need to progress?

*Charm is deceitful and beauty is passing,
But a woman who fears the Lord, she shall be praised.*

Proverbs 31:30

WHO AM I?

Who am I?
Beautiful and confident.

Who am I?
Strong and diligent.

Who am I?
Loving and disciplined.

Who am I?
Powerful and kind.

Who am I?
Wise and patient.

Who am I?
Positive and generous.

Who am I?
Respectful and delightful.

Who am I?
Faithful and humble.

Who am I?
Marvelously and wonderfully made.

Who am I?
A blessed child of God.

Therefore you shall be perfect, just as your Father in heaven is perfect.

Matthew 5:48

IT'S NOT ENOUGH

It is not enough to want something.
Unless I am willing to pursue it.

It is not enough to think I'll win.
Unless I am willing to be rejected.

It is not enough to want to teach.
Unless I am willing to be an example.

It is not enough to hear the truth.
Unless I am willing to accept it.

It is not enough to love someone.
Unless I am willing to love myself.

It is not enough to sacrifice for God.
Unless I am willing to obey Him.

It is not enough to talk the talk.
Unless I am willing to walk the walk.

I can do all things through Christ who strengthens me.

Philippians 4:13

A WOMAN OF GOD

Woman of God, you are a delight to meet.
Despite life's struggles, you have stayed sweet.

Please, tell me how you became so wise?
I seek the truth without any disguise.

Was it the pain you endured?
Did it make you strong and matured?

Or was it the tears in your eyes
When you had to fight all the lies?

Woman of God, you rewrote your life's story
With the Powerful Pen of Endurance and Glory.

I see that you rose beyond circumstances
And wisely used your God-given chances.

Woman of God, you made no excuse.
You chose the way the unsuccessful refuse.

You found the Key to Endless Opportunities,
And it opened the door to numerous possibilities.

Woman of God, I see the victory in your eyes.
Gone is all the pain, the struggle and strife.

You did not listen to the things you were told,
And now you sparkle and shine like pure gold.

Woman of God, you held on to your faith so tight
Even when it seemed to be like a struggle and fight.

You deserve to be respected, loved, and admired
By all the people whom you have truly inspired.

My dear sister, you are a genius indeed.
I think of you as such a beautiful breed.

Thank you for conquering the battles you fought.
Because of them, great lessons have been taught.

Woman of God, I must truthfully confess.
I am so proud of you and all your success.

Woman of God, you truly deserve a life of merit.
You have inspired many with your God-fearing spirit.

The Lord your God is He who goes with you, to fight for you against your enemies, to save you.

Deuteronomy 20:4

A MAN OF GOD

Man of God, you are a pleasure to meet.
I heard of the enemies you managed to defeat.

I can see the conqueror's look in your eyes.
Will you please tell me how you became so wise?

Was it the steep mountains you climbed?
Or the brutal battles you were assigned?

Maybe it was the strength you behold.
Did it help you fight so powerful and bold?

Whatever it was, your history speaks loudly.
I truly respect you, and with you I stand proudly.

Man of God, great wisdom you have displayed.
Even when you were hurt, and also betrayed.

I commend you for your great endurance and glory
And for sharing your powerful and inspiring life's story.

Just as you want men to do to you, you also do to them likewise.

Luke 6:31

EVERYDAY PEOPLE

The everyday people you meet,
And the everyday people on the street,

You see them as they walk,
And you hear them as they talk.

Take a look at their different cheekbones,
But do not frown at their distinctive skin tones.

Now, will you take a deeper look in their eyes?
You may be in for a shock and surprise.

Do you see they are from your same human race
Even though they may come from a different place?

Will you take some time to say "hello"?
Do not just rush along and quickly go.

Can you show them that you genuinely care
And share God's Word or even a prayer?

Remember the everyday people you meet
And that includes the everyday people on the street.

They are God's created people, like me
And God's created people, like you too.

Therefore I say to you, whatever things you ask when you pray, believe that you receive them, and you will have them.

Mark 11:24

I BELIEVE

I passionately believe with an unwavering devotion;
God's love for me is deeper and wider than the ocean.

I strongly believe, and I am fully persuaded;
Jesus is the Son of God, and I am converted.

I genuinely believe and also acknowledge;
God cares for me and gives me great knowledge.

I completely believe, and I undoubtedly recognize;
God's Word is the truth, and it can make me wise.

I clearly believe, accept, and also understand;
I am a child of God, and on His Rock I stand.

I believe, comprehend, and definitely know;
I am blessed enough, and I can certainly grow.

I joyfully believe, and I am unabashedly elated;
God will answer my prayers, and I will be elevated.

These things I have spoken to you, that in Me you may have peace. In the world you will have tribulation; but be of good cheer, I have overcome the world.

John 16:33

PEACE WITHIN

Do not force anything to happen,
But you should only allow.

When you let it go,
You will surely allow.

If you open your heart,
You will freely allow.

And many blessings will flow,
Because you have simply allowed.

The Lord is my shepherd; I shall not want.

Psalm 23:1

GOD'S BLESSINGS

God gives me everything I need.
God gives me everything to succeed.

God gives me everything in the physical.
God gives me everything in the spiritual.

God gives me everything I receive.
God gives me everything and I believe.

God gives me everything that is powerful.
God gives me everything that is wonderful.

God gives me everything in faith.
The God who gives me everything is Great!

God has not given us a spirit of fear, but of power and of love and of a sound mind.

2 Timothy 1:7

FEAR

Fear is truly an illusion.
Fear can create confusion.

Fear can make you scream.
Fear can kill your dream.

Fear can result in lack.
Fear can successfully attack.

Fear can help you hate.
Fear can force you to shake.

Fear can push you to run.
Fear can steal your fun.

Fear can cause you to be terrified.
Fear can leave you paralyzed.

But the only fear that can win,
Is the fear you willfully allow within.

Do not fear those who kill the body but cannot kill the soul. But rather fear Him who is able to destroy both soul and body in hell.

Matthew 10:28

FIRES OF HELL

I have been through the fires of Hell and back.
But the Lord has protected me.

I have been sick, hurt, and afflicted.
But the Lord has healed me.

I have been weak, tired, and worn.
But the Lord has strengthened me.

I have been hated, despised, and mistreated.
But the Lord has loved me.

I have been doubtful, unfaithful, and sinful.
But the Lord has forgiven me.

I have been attacked by the enemy.
But the Lord has rescued me.

I have been through the fires of Hell and back.
But the Lord has saved me.

Stand fast therefore in the liberty by which Christ has made us free, and do not be entangled again with a yoke of bondage.

Galatians 5:1

FREEDOM OF CHOICE

You gave me freedom of choice.
I choose my purpose, my task, my life.

You gave me freedom of choice.
I choose to be empowered with joy and love.

You gave me freedom of choice.
I choose Your wisdom, freedom, and peace.

You gave me freedom of choice.
I choose You as my Savior, Lord, and King.

I am not ashamed of the gospel of Christ, for it is the power of God to salvation for everyone who believes.

Romans 1:16(a)

GIVEN POWER

I have been given the power to know.
I am strong enough, and I can grow.

I have been given the power to be grand.
I will rise above and firmly take a stand.

I have been given the power to change.
I am ready to have my life rearrange.

I have been given the power to think.
My heart and mind can truly sync.

I have been given the power to win.
The race is on, so let us begin.

He who does not love does not know God, for God is love.

1 John 4:8

AMAZED!

Your wonderful love amazes me.
Your unmerited grace humbles me.

Your mighty power protects me.
Your great patience overwhelms me.

Your powerful wisdom fulfills me.
Your abundant blessings satisfy me.

Your perfect glory enlightens me.
Your selfless sacrifice saved me.

You are a chosen generation, a royal priesthood, a holy nation, His own special people, that you may proclaim the praises of Him who called you out of darkness into His marvelous light.

1 Peter 2:9

WHO ARE YOU?

Know who you are, O child of God.
You are royalty, truly special indeed.

Know who you are, O child of God.
A precious price for you He has paid.

Know who you are, O child of God.
Be joyful, thankful, humble, and happy.

Know who you are, O child of God.
Stay loving and gracious and always kind.

Know who you are, O child of God.
You were created for a delightful purpose.

Know who you are, O child of God.
You were made to fly high above the blue sky.

Therefore if the Son makes you free, you shall be free indeed.

John 8:36

BREATHE

Let it go, and just let God.
Let it go, despite the odd.

Let it go, release the pain.
Let it go, dance in the rain.

Let it go, and trust in Him.
Let it go, and smile within.

Let it go, start living again.
Let it go, there is much to gain.

Let it go, it is never too late.
Let it go, God's love is great.

Jesus said to them, "Because of your unbelief; for assuredly, I say to you, if you have faith as a mustard seed, you will say to this mountain, 'Move from here to there,' and it will move; and nothing will be impossible for you.

Matthew 17:20

CHALLENGES

Challenges come and challenges go.
Do not be defeated before fighting the foe.

Challenges come and challenges go.
You must have faith before you can grow.

Challenges come and challenges go.
Why should you quit and always say no?

Challenges come and challenges go.
Shun the social circle and status quo.

Challenges come and challenges go.
Trust in the Lord and let go of the woe.

Challenges come and challenges go.
Hold on tight and you will see the rainbow.

*The Lord takes pleasure in His people;
He will beautify the humble with salvation.*

Psalm 149:4

LOOK AT YOU!

Look at you!
Perfect and priceless.

Look at you!
Sweet and compassionate.

Look at you!
Gorgeous and beautiful.

Look at you!
Joyful and delightful.

Look at you!
Huggable and lovable.

Look at you!
Happy and confident.

Look at you!
God's work made into perfection!

Faith is the substance of things hoped for, the evidence of things not seen.

Hebrews 11:1

MEN OF OLD

The great men of old, I have been told,
Had treasured gifts we must behold.

They had a dream that would ignite.
Finding faith, would help them fight.

They knew the battle would be fierce and brutal
But would be far from being unsuccessful or futile.

So they chose to control their destiny
By humbly praying on bended knee.

They took responsibility for their actions
And made no excuses for any distractions.

The men of old understood fear was not an option.
They became bolder with every interaction.

Those wise men ignored all their negative critics
Who tried to berate them with hopeless statistics.

They did not give a moment's thought to quitting
Because for them, that would never be fitting.

They strategically planned out all of their actions
And fought their battles without any subtractions.

The men of old visualized what they would become
But they knew it would take much work and not fun.

They were compensated with numerous possibilities
And diligently used all their God-given opportunities.

They wisely used their tools and began to soar,
Flying on success like no one had before.

And when they embraced powerful faith,
Those men became like ravenous wraiths.

They were untouchable, unstoppable, and fearless
And were rewarded with much victory and greatness.

The great men of old, I have been told,
Had this valuable secret to behold.

They found that you must "see it" and "believe it"
Before you can actually "achieve it" and "receive it."

The thief does not come except to steal, and to kill, and to destroy. I have come that they may have life, and that they may have it more abundantly.

John 10:10

LIFE'S STORMS

Life's storm stirs up things.
Life's storm disaster brings.

Life's storm can cause us fright.
Life's storm is worth the fight.

Life's storm is always rough.
Life's storm will make us tough.

Life's storm will come and go.
Life's storm can help us grow.

Life's storm will never last.
Life's storm will come to pass.

"Be strong and do not let your hands be weak, for your work shall be rewarded!"

2 Chronicles 15:7

NEVER GIVE UP

I will hold on; I will hang on.
I will hold on tight with all my might.

I will hold on; I will hang on.
Though I hear doubts from others' mouths.

I will hold on; I will hang on.
The road is rough, but I will be tough.

I will hold on; I will hang on.
I must admit, I just cannot quit.

I will hold on; I will hang on.
My faith is strong it is never wrong.

I will hold on; I will hang on,
And my time will come to have some fun.

The Lord also will be a refuge for the oppressed, A refuge in times of trouble.

Psalm 9:9

GREATNESS

Greatness is given to me.
I will not be intimidated.

Greatness is given to me.
I will not compromise.

Greatness is given to me.
I will not be oppressed.

Greatness is given to me.
I will never fear.

Greatness is given to me.
I will be courageous.

Greatness is given to me.
I will succeed!

But as many as received Him, to them He gave the right to become children of God, to those who believe in His name.

John 1:12

I AM HIS

Standing in uniqueness.
I am.

An untouchable, faithful spirit.
I am.

Joy made in abundance.
I am.

A source of great power.
I am.

Loving, gentle, and kind.
I am.

Confident and wonderful.
I am.

Humble, delightful, and grateful.
I am.

God's breath made to perfection.
I am.

A child of the Mighty King.
I am.

Be still, and know that I am God.

Psalm 46:10(a)

BE STILL

Relax, do not worry, and just let it be.
Work hard, and in time you will truly see.

Believe that God can do anything.
So always trust Him with everything.

Make the best of your awakening moments.
And enjoy all of life's wonderful components.

Never be angry, nervous, or even anxious.
God's generosity is awesome and precious.

Therefore, make time and just relax.
Slow down, meditate, and simply ask.

Remember His Words, "Peace, be still."
And He has also said, "Follow My will."

To everything there is a season, a time for every purpose under heaven.

Ecclesiastes 3:1

LET IT GO

It is time to move on.
Release it now.

Your purpose was served.
Release it now.

It was for a short moment.
Release it now.

The season is over.
Release it now.

Your task is complete.
Release it now.

The lesson was learned.
Release it now.

He who believes and is baptized will be saved; but he who does not believe will be condemned.

Mark 16:16

LIFESAVER

I heard that You are powerful, O Thou.
I want to know You, please allow.
Bless me and show me just how.
I want to live for You, starting right now.

Good Lord, direct my path every day.
And shelter me from all evil, I pray.
Send Your angels to protect me today.
And guide me to do everything You say.

I want You to be the God of my life.
I need You in all my struggles and strife.
Please do not let my deeds become a rife.
I want to play the wonderful heavenly fife.

Be my Deliverer, Marvelous King, so grand.
When my enemies attack, please help me stand.
I need your mercy and grace to truly withstand.
I humbly ask for the help of Your powerful hand.

I have obeyed You, my Lord and Redeemer.
Help transform me to become a true believer.
From the day I was born, You made me an achiever.
So I will live by Your word, and I will be a receiver.

You are my awesome Master, Lord, and Savior.
You have taken away all my faults and my failure.
Thank You for Your boundless love and favor.
You will be forever my Generous Lifesaver.

*Keep your heart with all diligence,
For out of it spring the issues of life.*

Proverbs 4:23

TALK TO YOUR HEART

My dear heart, I know how much you care.
But why should you live in constant despair?

It is amazing to hear the movement of your beating.
And the sound of its rhythm is constantly repeating.

Please, let go of the hurt that you are now facing.
Replace it with the love of God you are wasting.

My precious heart, I am here to tell you today:
You must open your door to the beautiful day.

So, will you quit sighing and stop the constant crying?
And never give up, even though you feel like dying.

Watch, stand fast in the faith, be brave; be strong.

1 Corinthians 16:13

STAND UP!

Stand up with joy.
You are confident.

Stand up in faith.
You are a believer.

Stand up straight.
You are a worker.

Stand up strong.
You are a fighter.

Stand up tall.
You are a winner.

Stand up in wisdom.
You are an achiever.

Stand up in perfection.
You are a child of God.

Do not be deceived, God is not mocked; for whatever a man sows, that he will also reap.

Galatians 6:7

BOOMERANG

Life is like a boomerang.
The way you treat people
Is the same way you will be treated.
If you give them love or hate,
That is what you will get back.

Life is like a boomerang.
The things you say about people
Will be the same things said about you.
If you speak positively or negatively,
That is what you will get back.

Life is like a boomerang.
The way you see other people
Will be the same way you'll be viewed.
If you are thoughtful or prideful,
That is what you'll get back.

Life will always be like a boomerang.
All the things you do, say, and think
Are the exact things you will surely get back.
So, be loving, positive, and compassionate,
And that is what you will definitely get back.

You see then that a man is justified by works, and not by faith only.

James 2:24

TRUE SUCCESS

Success is an ongoing habit.
Success, you must be ready to grab it.

Success is a lifelong commitment.
Success is always being consistent.

Success is having faith and believing.
Success is setting goals and achieving.

Success is having strength and wisdom.
Success that is real gives us true freedom.

Success is learning how to be bold and daring.
Success is staying grounded when life is despairing.

Success is leaning on the Lord and knowing.
Success is believing in God and growing.

As obedient children, not conforming yourselves to the former lusts, as in your ignorance; [15]*but as He who called you is holy, you also be holy in all your conduct,* [16]*because it is written, "Be holy, for I am holy."*

1 Peter 1:14-16

THE FLOW

Some folks say I should go with the flow.
But I do not believe it must always be so.

Some folks say I should go with the flow.
But Mama said, "Be a leader and you'll grow."

Some folks say I should go with the flow.
But where it leads, I may never know.

Some folks say I should go with the flow.
But call me a rebel, and I will still say no!

Some folks say I should go with the flow.
But I do not want to live the status quo.

Some folks say I should go with the flow.
But it may take me to trouble or even a foe.

Some folks say I should go with the flow.
But I want my boat, so I can confidently row.

Some folks say I should go with the flow.
But I know only dead fish are carried like so!

Yet it shall not be so among you; but whoever desires to become great among you, let him be your servant.

Matthew 20:26

GREATNESS

There was a woman searching for greatness.
She thought she could purchase it with unkindness.
But she was bluntly told she needed meekness.
So she became angry, obnoxious, and clueless.

She thought a synonym for kindness was weakness
And tried to change love for strict unwillingness.
Then she became brainless, useless, and powerless
And was overtaken by madness and foolishness.

Therefore, when you are truly searching for greatness,
Never use negativity to replace righteousness.
Always follow the path of truthfulness and kindness
And dazzle all with your gentleness and sweetness.

The Lord is my rock and my fortress and my deliverer;
My God, my strength, in whom I will trust;
My shield and the horn of my salvation, my stronghold.

Psalm 18:2

TRUSTING GOD

Whatever you need,
Ask it of the Lord.

Whenever you pray,
Wait patiently on the Lord.

Whoever has hurt you,
Hand them to the Lord.

Whichever way you go,
Follow the Lord.

Wherever you live,
Reside in the Lord.

But thanks be to God, who gives us the victory through our Lord Jesus Christ.

1 Corinthians 15:57

VICTIM?

Why should I be a victim
When am a child of the most powerful King?

Why should I be a victim
When Jesus has died in my place?

Why should I be a victim
When He has wonderfully blessed me?

Why should I be a victim
When His love for me is awesome?

Why should I be a victim
When He has forgiven all my sins?

Why should I be a victim
When He is fighting all my battles?

Why should I be a victim
When He has angels watching over me?

Why should I be a victim
When I already know I am a victor?

God is faithful, by whom you were called into the fellowship of His Son, Jesus Christ our Lord.

1 Corinthians 1:9

GOD WANTS YOU!

What does God ask?
Everything of me.

What does God give?
Everything to me.

What does God expect?
Everything from me.

What does God want?
Everything for me.

What does God require?
Everything in me.

Let no one despise your youth, but be an example to the believers in word, in conduct, in love, in spirit, in faith, in purity.

1 Timothy 4:12

SMILE, SISTERS

Smile, sisters, smile.
Your life will flow like a stream.
If you follow your dream.

Smile, sisters, smile.
Always give your best.
And never settle for less.

Smile, sisters, smile.
Be the creator of your fate.
By changing your state.

Smile, sisters, smile.
The blue sky is the limit.
Grab your star, success is in it!

Therefore you also be ready, for the Son of Man is coming at an hour you do not expect.

Matthew 24:44

ARE YOU READY?

When you are ready,
You will truly know.
When you are ready,
Call and He will show.

When you are ready,
You will not have to cry.
When you are ready,
You will never ask why.

When you are ready,
You will make time to pray.
When you are ready,
You will see a brighter day.

When you are ready,
It will be your season.
When you are ready,
Ask and it will be given.

When you are ready,
Words will be spoken.
When you are ready,
The doors will be open.

When you are ready,
You will know it is time.
When you are ready,
Hope it will be fine.

So he answered and said, "You shall love the Lord your God with all your heart, with all your soul, with all your strength, and with all your mind,' and 'your neighbor as yourself."

Luke 10:27

LOVE ME!

When I sacrifice for others
And I forget who I am,
Who is going to love me?

When I give my absolute best
And all I get is a lot less,
Who is going to love me?

When I am feeling so blue
And I do not know what to do,
Who is going to love me?

When everything I have lost
And self-seeking comes at a cost,
Who is going to love me?

My God will say to me,
"My child, I love you!
But you must learn to love yourself."

"O Jerusalem, Jerusalem, the one who kills the prophets and stones those who are sent to her! How often I wanted to gather your children together, as a hen gathers her brood under her wings, but you were not willing!"

Luke 13:34

THE UNNOTICED

I walk and talk with them daily,
But they notice me only rarely.

I see their overflowing tears,
And I know of their terrible fears.

I wish they would speak with me
So I could help them to truly see.

I can show them how to be strong,
But they must not live in the wrong.

I would like them to really know
My love is pure and not a show.

I walk and talk with them every day,
But they ignore me in every single way.

—Jesus

He who does wrong will be repaid for what he has done, and there is no partiality.

Colossians 3:25 (NIV)

WRONG AND RIGHT

Wrong is wrong, and right is right.
You do not have to worry,
And you do not have to fight.

Wrong is wrong, and right is right.
Always speak the truth,
And your soul it will soothe.

Wrong is wrong, and right is right.
If you play by the rule,
You will not become a fool.

Wrong is wrong, and right is right.
Live by God's Word,
And retain what you have heard!

"I will be a Father to you, and you shall be My sons and daughters,
Says the Lord Almighty."

2 Corinthians 6:18

CHILD OF GOD

Child of God, be strong and brave.
God's work in you, He has displayed.
Have confidence and stand up tall.
And never worry that you will fall.

Child of God, have faith in Him.
He gave you strength so you can win.
Please work hard and do things well.
You will not just succeed but also excel.

Child of God, please speak the truth.
You knew it well when you were a youth.
Do not compromise the things you know.
The Awesome One has told you so.

Child of God, be good and kind.
He will give you joy and peace of mind.
So trust in Him and just believe.
All that you need, you will receive.

Child of God, walk in the Light.
You are protected by His power and might.
And when your life is not working right,
Reach out to Him and hold on tight.

Child of God, you must behave.
His life for you, He already gave.
So never worry about people's awful hate.
Work extremely hard and change your state.

Child of God, whom He loves to bless,
There is no need to fuss or to impress.
Never forget who you really are:
A child of the King of near and far.

Let no corrupt word proceed out of your mouth, but what is good for necessary edification, that it may impart grace to the hearers.

Ephesians 4:29

WORDS, WORDS, WORDS

"Words, words, words," sing the little wise birds.
"Be careful how you use your words."

Words that are uttered pure and whole,
These words will often touch the soul.

Words that are used as deceitful vice,
Such words will come with a great price.

Words that are uttered with power and might,
Those words can give us direction and light.

Words that carelessly and foolishly spoken,
Those words can cause friendships to be broken.

"Words, words, words," sing the little wise birds.
"Be careful how you use your daily words!"

Do not be conformed to this world, but be transformed by the renewing of your mind, that you may prove what is that good and acceptable and perfect will of God.

Romans 12:2

CHANGE

Father, please forgive me, I humbly pray.
And help me to do the things that You say.

Guide me to follow Your delightful way.
May I not repeat yesterday's mistakes today.

Lord, will you teach me how to forgive?
I want Your great blessings as long as I live.

Remove all the negative thoughts from my heart,
And replace them with positive ones as You ought.

Almighty God, give me a disciplined mind.
I yearn to be successful, delightful, and kind.

Allow me to see the world through Your eyes.
I want to distinguish the truth from all lies.

And finally, bless me with powerful faith to believe
That You will dwell in my heart and never will leave.

See then that you walk circumspectly, not as fools but as wise, ¹⁶redeeming the time, because the days are evil.

Ephesians 5:15-16

THE RIGHT TIME

Now is the time to become useful and truthful.
Now is the time to live for God and be faithful.

Now is the time to put away useless ignorance.
Now is the time to truly make a difference.

Now is the time to let God carry your load.
Now is the time to study His Holy Word.

Now is the time to let God fix your life that is broken.
Now is the time to obey the Words the Lord has spoken.

Let your eyes look straight ahead, and your eyelids look right before you.
²⁶Ponder the path of your feet, and let all your ways be established.
²⁷Do not turn to the right or the left; remove your foot from evil.

Proverbs 4:25-27

STAY FOCUSED

Stay focused on God, you people.
He is the Lord, Your Royal Highness.
He created you in awesome likeness.
And His love for you is truly priceless.

Stay focused on God, you people.
He knows your sorrow and pain.
He is your perfect sunshine and your rain.
And His blessings of joy you will attain.

Stay focused on God, you people.
Do not give up the struggle and fight.
Know that in life, God holds delight,
If you only hang on and never lose sight.

Stay focused on God, you people.
Praise and glorify His holy name.
Living truthfully for Him should be your aim,
And you will never see yourself the same again.

Stay focused on God, you people.
Trust Him in everything you do.
Remember, when you are feeling blue,
God has never lost His focus on you!

Praise the Lord from the heavens;
Praise Him in the heights!
²Praise Him, all His angels;
Praise Him, all His hosts!
³Praise Him, sun and moon;
Praise Him, all you stars of light!
⁴Praise Him, you heavens of heavens,
And you waters above the heavens!
⁵Let them praise the name of the Lord,
For He commanded and they were created.

Psalm 148:1(b)-5

PRAISE THE LORD!

Praise the Lord, all people, come now and rejoice.
Magnify Him for His blessings with a loud voice.

Honor God for designing all His awesome creation.
Bless Him ceaselessly, every country and every nation.

Venerate the powerful God for His mighty work.
Elevate Him for His awesome perfect handiwork.

Extol the Almighty for His profound greatness.
Glorify Him for His compassion and kindness.

Adore the Magnificent Lord, all His creatures alive.
Esteem Him with gladness, and you surely will thrive.

Laud Jehovah, as He delightfully guides your ways.
Cherish Him and be awed, astonished, and amazed!

Admire the Loving God and respect His glorious name.
Obey Him diligently and your life will never be the same.

Exalt the Heavenly Father, all angels and Heavenly host.
Revere Him for His wisdom, and in His excellence boast.

Hail the King of kings, speak of His righteousness.
Proclaim His holy and divine name, as well as His graciousness.

Celebrate the I Am for His love, compassion, and blessings.
Appreciate Him for answering your prayers without ceasing.

Adulate the true God, perfect rock and foundation.
Confess the name of Jesus, He is the true salvation.

Respect Elohim with all your mind, body, and soul.
Cherish Him for His mighty acts and you will be whole.

Call to Yahweh, who answers knocks at His door.
Adore Him who extends His grace to the poor.

Delight in the Lord's kindness, come and sing a new song.
Worship the Father, the Son, and the Holy Spirit all day long.

Abide in the Good Lord, there is nothing cleverer.
Thank Him whose perfect mercy endures forever.

I know that nothing is better for them than to rejoice, and to do good in their lives, ⁱ³and also that every man should eat and drink and enjoy the good of all his labor—it is the gift of God.

Ecclesiastes 3:12-13

LIVE YOUR LIFE!

Why are you wasting your life's precious years?
You have a dream, go pursue it!

Why are you wasting your life's precious years?
Life is great, open your eyes and see it!

Why are you wasting your life's precious years?
There is a world out there, go explore it!

Why are you wasting your life's precious years?
Life has been given to you, so embrace it!

Why are you wasting your life's precious years?
Be thankful for every day and enjoy it!

Why are you wasting your life's precious years?
Life is noticeably short, so learn to live it!

Therefore if the Son makes you free, you shall be free indeed.

John 8:36

FEARLESS FREEDOM

Lord, thank you for freeing me from my habitual mask.
I no longer have to pretend or cover up as I did in the past.
You created me wonderful, delightful, and powerful.
Therefore, I will be confident, grateful, and useful.

Father, help me to always remember who I am:
A child of the Almighty, the God of Abraham.
I pray to always please You, most powerful King.
I am grateful to have a beautiful song to sing.

I am no longer addicted to clothes, purses, jewelry, and cars.
I do not have the need for fake friends, substance abuse, or bars.
Whoever wants to be in my life must truly understand,
I am incredibly happy, confident, and fearless where I stand.

Take me or leave me, the choice is yours to make.
I know I am made in God's image and am not a mistake.
I will not disguise myself, be fake, or pretend anymore.
God has blessed me with all I need, and even much more!

Here is what I have seen: It is good and fitting for one to eat and drink, and to enjoy the good of all his labor in which he toils under the sun all the days of his life which God gives him; for it is his heritage.

Ecclesiastes 5:18

ROCK THE WORLD

I want to rock the world before I die.
I will not complain, nor will I cry.
I will set my goals and dreams exceedingly high.
And I will soar far above the great blue sky.

I want to rock the world before I die.
Lord, do not let me go with my music still inside.
Let me taste a slice of life's Victory Pie.
I know I am not worthy, but I will continue to try.

I want to rock the world before I die.
I was not born to just eat, live, and survive.
I am here for a purpose, a plan, and to thrive.
So I will shout, "World, here I am and am alive!"

I want to rock the world before I die.
I will play my guitar with passion and electrify.
And before I close my eyes and say "goodbye,"
I will praise the Lord for letting me amplify!

Let us hear the conclusion of the whole matter:
Fear God and keep His commandments,
For this is man's all.
¹⁴For God will bring every work into judgment,
Including every secret thing, whether good or evil.

Ecclesiastes 12:13-14

LAST BREATH

Before I take my last breath, I will say,
"I lived my life with all my might."

Before I take my last breath, I will say,
"I enjoyed my time, and I have shined."

Before I take my last breath, I will say,
"I aimed so high, I touched the sky."

Before I take my last breath, I will say,
"I fought the good fight with all of my might."

Before I take my last breath, I will say,
"Lord, I am blessed, and world, goodbye!"

He who did not spare His own Son, but delivered Him up for us all, how shall He not with Him also freely give us all things?

Romans 8:32

GOD'S PROMISES

I promise to love you.
I promise to heal you.

I promise to answer you.
I promise to support you.

I promise to comfort you.
I promise to deliver you.

I promise to forgive you.
I promise to restore you.

I promise to provide for you.
I promise to never leave you.

I promise you eternal life.
I promise to keep My promises.

—God

But certainly God has heard me;
He has attended to the voice of my prayer.

Psalm 66:19

ANSWERED PRAYERS

Mighty and Awesome God, You can move any mountain.
You bless us abundantly, whether it is in sunshine or rain.

When we approached You, we were walking in much darkness.
But You gave us Your True Light and removed all our sadness.

Lord, Your perfect mercy surpasses all forms of understanding.
And You have truly transformed our life and made it outstanding.

You heard our call, when no one listened to our voices.
You have blessed and empowered us with many choices.

You dried every tear from our tired and crying eyes.
And You unleashed our feet from all ungodly ties.

You lifted us up, when we could hardly stand.
And You placed our feet firmly on solid land.

You kept us safe until the raging storms passed by.
Now we can spread our wings and truly fly high.

You shined Your Light, and now we can clearly see.
We will surrender our hearts and souls only to Thee.

Lord, we will forever praise, honor, and thank You.
For all the wonderful things that You always do.

We will lift up Your Holy, Awesome, and Divine name.
For our life You have changed; it will never be the same.

Powerful, Marvelous, Generous, and Sovereign King.
You have put in our mouths a happy song to sing.

We praise, honor, thank, and exalt You, now and forever.
We offer our prayers, and for Your blessings we endeavor.

Thank You for listening to our supplications and plea.
Our chains have been broken, and we are set free.

Almighty, Perfect, Awesome God of our salvation.
We are believers, and to You we submit our oration.

In My Father's house are many mansions; if it were not so, I would have told you. I go to prepare a place for you.

John 14:2

A GLIMPSE OF HEAVEN

"Come with me, child of God" a gentle voice uttered to me."
There is an awesome and delightful place, I'd like you to see.
Although I was very hesitant in obeying his strange command.
I gently closed my eyes and held on to his powerful right hand.

It was a few moments later, when he said, "open your eyes."
When I did, I was dumbfounded by a delightful surprise.
Then, he said, "Look all around, and speak loud about what you see."
But I couldn't because I was awed by what saw; I fell to my knee.

After a while, I started to speak with much reverence and respect.
I said, "This is a perfect country—one I did not imagine or expect.
It is lovelier than the one I used to dream of for a very long time.
Its beauty and richness are so awesome; there is not even a crime!

Also, I see the unity of all people, every ethnic, race, nation, and color.
And I can see heavenly beings and all God's faithful ones in multicolor.
And I can hear their sweet melodious voices, singing in one accord.
They're dressed in white robes, praising and worshipping their God.

I recognize the beautiful song they are singing, "No Tears in Heaven."
I see a throne, and around it are lighted lamps, and there are seven.
Then an angel whispered, "No more sorrow pain, dying, or crying."
"There's perfect joy, laughter, and everything pure and gratifying."

I said, "Twelve gates of the city—each made of one perfect pearl. Wow!"
The streets are like glass paved in pure gold. I couldn't help but to bow.
When I walked in, I saw a wall of precious stones; its riches blinded me.
It was made of jasper, sapphire, agate, and emerald; what a delight to see.

Then, the angel said, "Come. There are more things you must still see."
And he guided me to "The River of The Water of Life;" it flowed so free.
It brightly shinned as it passed through the throne of God and the Lamb.
"The Tree of Good and Evil" from Eden on both sides, planted by I Am.

As we continued, I became fearful because I didn't know what lay ahead.
But the angel said, "Fear not. God's name is written on your forehead."
Then, like a trumpet, a voice said, "Come here." He looked like Jasper.
Then, He said to me, "The righteous shall live here forever and prosper."

He continued with "Come up to see the place We've prepared for you.
It's a home created for you and everyone who has lived a faithful life too.
I'll not be ashamed to be called your God. I Am happy you are My child.
This great city was built for the faithful; those who are with Me will be reconciled."

I was having such a time; I had to praise Him for a magnificent creation.
"Holy, Holy, Holy! You are All Mighty, Most Perfect and Great One!"
I saw the children of God, perfectly adorned and beautiful as a bride.
And a voice said to them, "Welcome home, children; come in and with Me, abide."

Therefore I also, after I heard of your faith in the Lord Jesus and your love for all the saints, ¹⁶do not cease to give thanks for you, making mention of you in my prayers: ¹⁷that the God of our Lord Jesus Christ, the Father of glory, may give to you the spirit of wisdom and revelation in the knowledge of Him, ¹⁸the eyes of your understanding being enlightened; that you may know what is the hope of His calling, what are the riches of the glory of His inheritance in the saints.

Ephesians 1:15-18

101 ENLIGHTENING THOUGHTS

1. Be enlightened to know God.
2. Be enlightened to know yourself.
3. Be enlightened to be positive.
4. Be enlightened to ignore the critics.
5. Be enlightened to have self-esteem.
6. Be enlightened to trust God.
7. Be enlightened to choose good friends.
8. Be enlightened to love your enemies.
9. Be enlightened to apologize when necessary.
10. Be enlightened to avoid prideful disputes.
11. Be enlightened to inspire young people.
12. Be enlightened to care for the elderly.
13. Be enlightened to live each day as your last.
14. Be enlightened to be thankful every day.
15. Be enlightened to be fearless.
16. Be enlightened to have powerful faith.
17. Be enlightened to have a dream.
18. Be enlightened to be a diligent worker.
19. Be enlightened to love yourself.
20. Be enlightened to be different.
21. Be enlightened to make time for yourself.
22. Be enlightened to make time for your family.
23. Be enlightened to make time for friends.
24. Be enlightened to help the poor and needy.
25. Be enlightened to do missionary work.
26. Be enlightened to read God's Word.
27. Be enlightened to teach God's Word.
28. Be enlightened to leave vengeance to God.
29. Be enlightened to love your neighbor.
30. Be enlightened to have self-respect.

31. Be enlightened to respect others.
32. Be enlightened to have godly wisdom.
33. Be enlightened to do God's will.
34. Be enlightened to make fervent prayers.
35. Be enlightened to be gentle.
36. Be enlightened to make time alone.
37. Be enlightened to shun negativity.
38. Be enlightened to make your own decisions.
39. Be enlightened to enjoy nature.
40. Be enlightened to praise God.
41. Be enlightened to stick to your commitments.
42. Be enlightened to take care of your responsibilities.
43. Be enlightened to live a happy life.
44. Be enlightened to be true to yourself.
45. Be enlightened to be honest.
46. Be enlightened to strive for excellence.
47. Be enlightened to be optimistic.
48. Be enlightened to have integrity.
49. Be enlightened to be a dedicated person.
50. Be enlightened to seek unlimited possibilities.
51. Be enlightened to appreciate time.
52. Be enlightened to practice politeness.
53. Be enlightened to be kind to strangers.
54. Be enlightened to strive for quality, rather than quantity.
55. Be enlightened to be reliable.
56. Be enlightened to laugh often.
57. Be enlightened to have good work ethics.
58. Be enlightened to spread joy.
59. Be enlightened to stand up for something worthwhile.
60. Be enlightened to be friendly.
61. Be enlightened to be humble.
62. Be enlightened to be compassionate.
63. Be enlightened to serve others.

64. Be enlightened to enjoy the simple things of life.
65. Be enlightened to be spontaneous.
66. Be enlightened to take worthy risks.
67. Be enlightened to be confident.
68. Be enlightened to help the innocent.
69. Be enlightened to be spiritually minded.
70. Be enlightened to care of your health.
71. Be enlightened to pursue peace.
72. Be enlightened to learn something new every day.
73. Be enlightened to share your blessings.
74. Be enlightened to examine your character.
75. Be enlightened to forgive others.
76. Be enlightened to forgive yourself.
77. Be enlightened to be patient with others.
78. Be enlightened to taste your words.
79. Be enlightened to use your talents to help others.
80. Be enlightened to make a difference in this world.
81. Be enlightened to be kind to animals.
82. Be enlightened to improve yourself.
83. Be enlightened to know when to say no.
84. Be enlightened to be thankful for every day.
85. Be enlightened to motivate others.
86. Be enlightened to handle stress effectively.
87. Be enlightened to pray for everyone.
88. Be enlightened to stay away from gossips.
89. Be enlightened to take time for meditation.
90. Be enlightened to give without reproach.
91. Be enlightened to write your story.
92. Be enlightened to obey God's Word.
93. Be enlightened to get to see the world.
94. Be enlightened to see the good in others.
95. Be enlightened to never give up.
96. Be enlightened to know when to speak up.

97. Be enlightened to know when to be quiet.
98. Be enlightened to be generous.
99. Be enlightened to stand up for the truth.
100. Be enlightened to serve God.
101. Be enlightened to make it to Heaven.

These things I have written to you who believe in the name of the Son of God, that you may know that you have eternal life, and that you may continue to believe in the name of the Son of God.

1 John 5:13

THE ENLIGHTENED LETTER

Dear _____ (your name here),

My love for you sparkles brighter than you can comprehend.
I have created a dazzling Mansion for you, a place to ascend.
If you trust in My Word, you will be brilliant, and you will transcend.
But first, you must become My shining star, and also My true friend.
I will not turn off your flicker, nor will I hide My sunshine from you.
I am the True Light that illuminates every good thing that you do.
I will brighten your dark nights and add shimmer to your days too.
But you must trust Me with everything that is splendorous and true.
I knew you when you were a twinkle in your mother's womb.
I am the Brightness who created you: know Me, do not just assume.
I saw the warm glow in you from child to adult and now you bloom.
I am the Resplendent Energy that will walk with you even to the tomb.
I can radiate your paths and lengthen every minute of your day.
But you must be willing to be fired up to do the things that I say.
If you welcome Me into your heart, there I will shine, and I will stay.
And I will be your abundance of blessings, especially when you pray.

—Almighty God

The Lord is good to all, and His tender mercies are over all His works.

Psalm 145:9

THE RESILIENT CLOSING

Friends, I hope this encouraging poem book has touched your soul, empowered you to seek a goal, evoked you to stay in control, and enlightened you to be made whole.

It is my greatest desire, that your sorrows change into joy, your defeats into victory, and your failures into accomplishments.

And when life presents itself to you as roller coasters of unmanageable sorrows, unexpected sicknesses, and unpredictable failures, you will prevail through your powerful faith in the Almighty God. Believe that He is the only One who can fix your mess, relieve your stress, and heal your distress.

Additionally, strive to attain a meaningful life by pleasing God with prayer, reading His Word, and applying it to your life and you will be greatly rewarded with His great blessings.

It is my earnest wish that you embrace humility, hold on to kindness, and passionately seek after true happiness. I pray that *Poems for Hungry Souls* assists in brightening your day, inspiring your soul, and enlightening your life.

Remember to smile with great confidence because you can *"Trust in the* L*ORD* *with all your heart, And lean not on your own understanding; In all your ways acknowledge Him, And He shall direct your paths"* Proverbs 3:5-6.

ABOUT THE AUTHOR

Jeannie Colon is the author of the following books: *Enlighten Your Life* and *The Successful Journey of Prayer*.

She is also a poet, motivational speaker, and keynote speaker. Additionally, she is a member of Toastmasters International.

Jeannie has been a Christian for more than forty years. She has touched the lives of many by sharing God's Word.

Along with her undeniable love and passion for God, she is blessed to live in Florida, close to her daughter, her son-in-law, and her grandchildren.

Learn more about Jeannie Colon.
enlightenedwomanofGod.com
Facebook: Jeannie Colon The Author

www.ingramcontent.com/pod-product-compliance
Lightning Source LLC
Chambersburg PA
CBHW071228080526
44587CB00013BA/1537